THE ART OF EXPLANATION FOR WOMAN

Unraveling the Mysteries of Communication With Women

Scott M. Curtis

Copyright ©Scott M. Curtis
2023

This book is intended for informational purposes only and is not a substitute for professional advice or guidelines. The author and publisher disclaim any liability arising from the use of the information provided in this book.

TABLE OF CONTENTS

CONFLICT RESOLUTION AND PROBLEM-SOLVING

- Handling Disagreements
- Problem-Solving Strategies
- The Importance of Compromise

COMMUNICATING IN RELATIONSHIPS

- Communication In Romantic Relationships
- Communication with friends and family
- Building Stronger Connections

WORKPLACE COMMUNICATION

- Women In The Professional World
- Effective communication at work
- Navigating Office Dynamics

DIGITAL COMMUNICATION AND SOCIAL MEDIA

- Communication In The Digital Age
- Social media and online etiquette
- Maintaining Healthy Digital Relationships

UNDERSTANDING FEMALE PERSPECTIVES

- Breaking Stereotypes
- Intersectionality and Diversity
- The Power of Inclusivity

EMPOWERING WOMEN THROUGH COMMUNICATION

- Building Confidence
- Leadership and Communication

- Inspiring Change

CONCLUSION

INTRODUCTION

Welcome to the World of Communication

Communication is the cornerstone of our existence as human beings. It's a large and intricate universe where words, gestures, expressions, and even silences retain great significance. In this introductory chapter, we go on a trip into the heart of communication, with a special focus on solving the mysteries of speaking with women.

Why is understanding communication so vital, especially in the context of women? The solution resides in the range and depth of human experiences. Women, like men, have unique ideas, emotions, and ways of expressing themselves. By plunging into this environment, we empower ourselves with the tools to build meaningful friendships, resolve problems, and inspire change.

Throughout this book, we will study the nuances of female communication, from the subtleties of nonverbal clues to the skill of emotional intelligence. We'll delve into the intricacies of speaking her language and managing various forms of relationships, from personal to professional. Moreover, we'll address the impact of digital communication and the value of comprehending other perspectives.

As we walk farther into this adventure, bear in mind that the purpose is not to generalize or stereotype but to promote empathy, respect, and inclusivity. We hope that, at the end of this book, you'll not only have a better knowledge of effective communication with women but also a heightened appreciation for the richness of various human interactions. So, let's begin this expedition together and discover the art of explanation for women.

Why Understanding Women's Communication Matters

Communication is the essence of human contact, and knowing how various individuals express themselves is vital. In this chapter, we look into the necessity of comprehending women's communication patterns and why it holds particular value.

1.Promoting Authentic Connections: When we understand and respect how women communicate, we clear the path for more authentic and lasting connections. It's through excellent communication that we can actually come to know one another, create trust, and forge solid relationships. By embracing and supporting varied communication methods, we create a society where women feel heard and understood.

2.   Resolving   Misunderstandings:
Miscommunications and misunderstandings can
lead to conflict, strained relationships, and
missed   opportunities.   By   gaining   an
understanding of the distinctive elements of
women's communication, we may lessen these
impediments. It allows us to explain goals,
resolve disagreements, and build harmony in
diverse circumstances, whether at home, in
business, or in social circles.

3.   Empowering   Women: Understanding
women's communication is a vital step towards
empowerment. It acknowledges the relevance of
their voices and viewpoints. When women feel
that their opinions and feelings are appreciated,
it bolsters their self-esteem and encourages them
to take an active role in decision-making
processes, both in personal and professional
contexts.

4. Inclusivity and Equality: In a world that
cherishes   diversity   and   gender   equality,
comprehending women's communication is
pivotal. It breaks down misconceptions and
addresses biases that might inhibit success.
Embracing and valuing varied communication
styles creates a more inclusive society where

everyone has a voice and an opportunity to be heard.

5. Enhanced Problem-Solving: Effective communication is at the basis of successful problem-solving. By knowing women's communication patterns, we may work together more efficiently to address complicated situations. This leads to inventive solutions and a more productive, cooperative environment.

6. Personal Growth: On an individual level, learning to comprehend and adapt to varied communication styles, including those of women, may be a transformative experience.

It sharpens our empathy, emotional intelligence, and adaptability, making us better communicators and better people.

Understanding women's communication is not about generalizing or stereotyping but about acknowledging the multiplicity of voices and viewpoints in the world. It's about cultivating inclusivity, developing empathy, and ultimately building a culture where every individual, regardless of their gender, feels appreciated, understood, and empowered. As we go deeper into the art of explanation for women, keep these ideas in mind, for they underpin the essence of our trip.

THE FOUNDATIONS OF FEMALE COMMUNICATION

Understanding Gender And Communication

Communication is a crucial component of human connection, and it's influenced by a wide range of circumstances, including gender. In this chapter, we explore the complicated interplay between gender and communication and how knowing this link might deepen our ability to communicate with one another.

1 Gender as a Social Construct: Gender is not a fixed biological attribute; it is a social construct that spans a vast spectrum of identities and

manifestations. Understanding this is the first step in appreciating the range of communication methods. By acknowledging that gender is more than just a binary concept, we open ourselves to a world of varied viewpoints.

2. Cultural and Societal Influences: Culture and society play a huge role in defining how individuals, particularly women, communicate. Social conventions, expectations, and traditions affect the way women express themselves. Recognizing these influences allows us to contextualize and appreciate the complex tapestry of communication styles.

3. Verbal vs. nonverbal communication: Men and women may demonstrate variances in verbal and nonverbal communication. While some women may use more oblique language or complex phrasing, others may communicate more directly. It's vital to avoid making sweeping generalizations and instead focus on individual communication preferences.

4. Emotional Expression: Women, in many countries, may be encouraged to express emotions more openly than men. Understanding these societal influences can help us create safe

spaces for emotional expression, allowing for better and more real connections.

5. Listening and Empathy: Women generally excel in active listening and empathetic communication. Acknowledging this strength can lead to more fruitful talks, as active listening is vital for creating trust and understanding.

Overcoming gender preconceptions: Gender preconceptions can lead to miscommunication and bias. By questioning and overcoming these prejudices, we may create an open, courteous, and meaningful discourse. This not only benefits women but also contributes to a more inclusive society for everyone.

7. Intersectionality: Gender is merely one dimension of an individual's identity. It connects with other elements, such as race, sexuality, and socioeconomic status. Recognizing these intersections is key to appreciating the complexity of communication styles.

Understanding gender and communication is about embracing variety and valuing individuality. It's about realizing the influence of culture and society on communication styles and attempting to overcome biases and stereotypes.

By doing so, we build a world where everyone's voice is appreciated and every individual, regardless of their gender, is empowered to communicate truthfully. As we continue our exploration into the art of explanation for women, let's keep these insights in mind, as they form the cornerstone of more successful and inclusive communication.

The Power of Listening

Listening is an often undervalued yet deeply powerful part of effective communication. It is the unsung hero of understanding, connecting, and developing meaningful connections. In this section, we will look into the transforming power of listening and how it may greatly impact your capacity to communicate, especially in the context of women.

1 Creating a Safe Environment: When we sincerely listen, we create a safe and open environment for the other person to express themselves. This is especially critical when talking with women, since they may encounter societal constraints that urge them to be more reserved. By being a good listener, you allow women to communicate their thoughts and feelings without judgment or interruption.

2. Fostering Understanding: Listening is the key to understanding. It goes beyond simply hearing words; it entails paying attention to nonverbal signs, emotions, and the underlying meaning behind the words said. Women, like everyone else, have complex ideas and feelings. By listening actively, you can obtain deeper insights into their perspectives.

3. Building Trust: Trust is the foundation of any great connection. Listening is a critical component of trust-building. When women feel heard and understood, trust naturally builds. This trust leads to more open and honest communication, which is vital in personal and professional encounters.

4. Empathy and Validation: Listening with empathy allows you to affirm the feelings and experiences of the person you're interacting with. This is particularly crucial when engaging with women, as they may encounter distinct issues and experiences. Empathetic listening reassures them that their experiences and emotions are respected.

5. Resolving Conflict: Effective listening is a key technique for conflict resolution. When you

actively listen to the problems and frustrations of women, it becomes simpler to handle and resolve conflicts in a constructive manner. Listening enables compromise and collaborative problem-solving.

6. own growth: Being a good listener is not only useful for those you converse with; it also adds to your own growth. It boosts your emotional intelligence, communication abilities, and adaptability. You become a more understanding and empathetic person in all areas of your life.

7. Equalizing the Conversation: In some circumstances, women's voices may be neglected or overlooked. By being a proactive listener, you can help guarantee that women's voices are heard and appreciated equally, leading to a more inclusive and balanced discourse.

The power of listening cannot be overemphasized. It is a cornerstone of efficient communication, a tool for creating trust and understanding, and a crucial part of empowering women to express themselves. As you continue on your adventure to discover the mysteries of communication with women, remember that being an attentive and empathic listener is a talent that may revolutionize the way you connect and interact with the women in your life.

Nonverbal Communication Cues

Nonverbal communication is a universal language that transcends words and tells volumes about our thoughts, feelings, and intentions. This silent type of expression includes body language, facial emotions, gestures, and tone of voice. In the context of communication, nonverbal clues are as significant, if not more so, than the words we pick. Here's why:

1 Unspoken Truths: Nonverbal clues often reveal what words conceal. They provide insight into a person's feelings, attitudes, and honesty. When speaking with women, noticing these indicators will help you grasp the underlying feelings that may not be overtly articulated.

2. Emotional Insights: Facial expressions and body language transmit a variety of emotional information. Understanding these indicators allows you to respond with better empathy and

support, especially when women might be hesitant to convey their feelings vocally.

3. Building rapport: Matching your nonverbal cues to those of the person you're interacting with can help build rapport and trust. It generates a sense of connection and understanding that goes beyond spoken words.

4. Clarifying Intentions: Nonverbal indicators can clarify the intentions underlying a message. For instance, a friendly grin might soothe a challenging talk, whereas crossed arms may signal defensiveness. By being attuned to these signs, you can adapt your speech to produce more beneficial outcomes.

5. Cultural Awareness: Nonverbal cues might vary among cultures, so it's necessary to be culturally sensitive. When interacting with women from varied backgrounds, acknowledging these differences can avoid

misunderstandings and create polite conversations.

6. Active Listening: Nonverbal clues are crucial to active listening. They show that you're fully involved in the discourse, reinforcing that the speaker's remarks are valuable.

7. Conflict Resolution: Nonverbal cues can de-escalate or exacerbate confrontations. When speaking with women, especially in stressful situations, your nonverbal cues can play a vital role in providing a secure and respectful environment for settlement.

In summary, nonverbal communication cues are a valuable tool in the art of explanation for women. They provide a deeper understanding of emotions, help in creating trust, and boost the overall quality of communication. By refining your ability to both read and express nonverbal clues, you may become a more effective and sympathetic communicator, increasing your relationships and connections.

SPEAKING HER LANGUAGE

Building Rapport

Rapport is the foundation of any effective encounter, conversation, or relationship. It's the connection, trust, and mutual understanding that provide a comfortable and open place for conversation. When it comes to speaking with women, creating rapport is vital for fostering meaningful and respectful interactions.

The Importance of Rapport:

1 Trust and Comfort: Building rapport with women, like with everyone, establishes trust and comfort. It allows people to feel at ease and protected during the talk, which is particularly vital in sensitive or personal discussions.

2. Open and Honest Communication: When rapport is good, individuals are more likely to talk openly and honestly. This involves sharing thoughts, feelings, and viewpoints without fear of criticism or misunderstanding.

3. Enhanced Empathy: Building rapport typically entails active listening and displaying empathy. This not only helps you better grasp the other person's position but also encourages them to consider yours.

4. Dispute Resolution: In times of dispute or disagreement, a solid rapport can be a lifeline. It provides a platform for courteous and constructive interactions, which are vital for resolving conflicts and maintaining healthy relationships.

Effective Strategies for Building Rapport:

1 Active Listening: Pay attentive attention to what the other person is saying. Show that you are totally involved in the conversation by maintaining eye contact, nodding, and delivering verbal clues like "I understand" or "Tell me more."

2. Empathetic Responses: Respond to their emotions and experiences with empathy. Acknowledge their feelings and express understanding. For example, "I can see that this situation is frustrating for you."

3. Ask Open-Ended Questions: Encourage deeper conversations by asking open-ended questions that need more than a simple yes or no response. This invites people to talk more about their thoughts and feelings.

4. Find Common Ground: Discover shared hobbies, experiences, or values that can help develop a sense of connection. Highlighting

these commonalities generates a feeling of togetherness.

5. Respect Boundaries: Be cognizant of personal boundaries and respect the other person's comfort level. Everyone has their own pace in creating rapport, and it's crucial to respect their space and preferences.

6. Consistency: Building rapport is a constant effort. It demands consistency and real interest in preserving the relationship. Regularly check in and show that you cherish the connection.

7. Authenticity: Be yourself. Authenticity is crucial to creating meaningful rapport. People admire authenticity and are more likely to trust and connect with someone who is real.

Remember that rapport is not just a one-time effort; it's a constant process that strengthens over time. Whether in personal relationships, business situations, or informal discussions, good rapport-building is a vital skill for increasing communication and connection, especially when speaking with women.

The Art of Expressing Yourself

The ability to communicate effectively is a cornerstone of meaningful communication. It's an art that entails presenting your thoughts, emotions, and ideas in a way that is clear, honest, and respectful. When it comes to interacting with women, learning this art is particularly vital, as it creates the door for open and real discussion. Here's why mastering the art of expressing oneself matters:

The Significance of Expressing Yourself:

1 Authenticity: Expressing yourself authentically implies being true to your views and feelings. It lets you communicate with authenticity and integrity, establishing trust in your connections.

2. Clarity: Effective self-expression guarantees that your message is clear and easily comprehended. It minimizes misconceptions and paves the way for fruitful communication.

3. Emotional Connection: Expressing emotions, both positive and negative, helps develop emotional bonds. Sharing your feelings and listening to others' emotions is an important component of human contact.

4. Conflict Resolution: When you can express your opinions and concerns quietly and respectfully, it becomes simpler to resolve disagreements and work through problems, especially when dealing with women.

5. Respect and Empathy: Expressing yourself respectfully and empathetically implies that you value the other person's opinion. It enables a two-way exchange of ideas and builds understanding.

Guidelines for Mastering the Art of Expression:

1 Self-awareness: Before you can express yourself successfully, it's vital to comprehend your own thoughts and feelings. Take time to focus on what you want to express and why.

2. Clarity and Brevity: Be clear and succinct in your speech. Avoid superfluous jargon or lengthy explanations. Let your point be ststraightforward.

3. Active Listening: Communication is a two-way street. Listening to the other person's answer and altering your expression based on their feedback is a critical aspect of effective communication.

4. Honesty: Honesty is vital to creating trust. Be sincere in your expressions, but also be conscious of how your words may affect the other person.

5. Empathy: Try to grasp the perspective and emotions of the person you're interacting with.

This lets you customize your expression to their wants and feelings.

6. Positive and negative feelings: Don't shy away from expressing both positive and negative feelings. It's healthy to communicate your delight and enthusiasm, as well as your concerns, frustrations, and fears. Doing so helps promote well-rounded and open conversation.

7. Respect Boundaries: Recognize the comfort levels and boundaries of the individual you're interacting with. Be attentive to their emotional condition and adapt your expression accordingly.

8. Practice and Feedback: Like any art, mastering the art of expression needs practice. Seek input from reputable people to develop your communication abilities.

As you embark on the adventure of decoding the mysteries of communication with women, realize that the art of expressing oneself is a skill that evolves with time and experience. It's about finding the balance between self-expression and care for the other person and cultivating a communication style that is both honest and compassionate.

Effective Tone and Word Choice

In the field of communication, the way you deliver your words can be as effective as the message itself. Tone and word choice are two key components that impact the success of your communication, especially when connecting with women. Let's discuss why mastering effective tone and word choice is vital and how to do it:

The Importance of Effective Tone and Word Choice:

1 Respect and empathy: Your tone and word choice set the tone for the conversation. Using courteous and empathic language communicates that you value the other person's feelings and views. It promotes a sense of mutual regard and understanding.

2. Clarity and Understanding: The correct tone and word choice enhance the clarity of your message. When your words connect with your intent and feelings, it's easier for the other person to comprehend you. Ambiguity and misunderstanding are decreased.

3. Conflict Resolution: In conflicts or disagreements, the correct tone and word choice can de-escalate a situation and facilitate fruitful communication. They help establish an environment where differences can be expressed politely.

4. Positive Relationships: Positive tone and word choice contribute to creating and maintaining healthy relationships. They establish a sense of trust and appreciation, reinforcing the cornerstone of every genuine connection.

Guidelines for Mastering Effective Tone and Word Choice:

1 Empathetic Language: Use language that recognizes the other person's perspective and feelings. Express empathy and understanding, even when you disagree.

2. Avoid Negative Assumptions: Steer clear of making negative assumptions about the other person's motives or sentiments. Give them the benefit of the doubt and seek clarification if needed.

3. Active Listening: Pay attention to the other person's words and modify your tone and word choice based on their cues and emotions. This displays active engagement in the conversation.

4. Consider the setting: Adapt your tone and word choice to the context. Conversations in informal contexts may have distinct conventions compared to professional or formal situations.

5. Respect Boundaries: Recognize and respect personal boundaries. Avoid invasive or offensive language and be attentive to cultural or individual differences.

6. Use "I" phrases: When expressing personal ideas or feelings, use "I" phrases to accept responsibility for your perspective. For example, say, "I feel that..." don't say "You make me feel..."

7. Positive Language: Whenever feasible, phrase your statements in a positive manner. Emphasize solutions and cooperation above criticism or blame.

8. Avoid Stereotypes and Generalizations: Be mindful not to employ stereotypes or broad generalizations, especially when communicating with women. Recognize individuality and variety.

9. Proofread and revise: Written communication, such as emails or texts, allows you to evaluate and revise your tone and word choice. Take the effort to ensure your written communication expresses your desired message.

10. Seek Feedback: Solicit feedback from others to examine how effectively your tone and word choice correspond with your aims and the impact they have on your communication.

Mastering appropriate tone and word choice is a continual practice that involves self-awareness and continuous refining. As you explore the art of explanation for women, remember that your choice of words and tone may be a strong weapon for generating polite, meaningful, and fruitful conversations.

CONFLICT RESOLUTION AND PROBLEM-SOLVING

Handling Disagreements

Disagreements are a natural aspect of any relationship or encounter, and how we handle them can dramatically affect the result of a debate. When it comes to speaking with women, learning the skill of addressing conflicts is vital, as it helps to foster respectful and constructive interactions. This why it matters and how to do it properly:

The Significance of Handling Disagreements:

1 Maintaining regard: How you negotiate arguments displays your regard for the other

person's perspective. By handling differences with understanding and empathy, you reinforce the worth of their viewpoints.

2. Conflict Resolution: Disagreements are often the catalyst for growth and progress. Addressing them constructively can lead to better solutions and a deeper understanding of each other's opinions.

3. Strengthening Relationships: Successfully addressing conflicts can lead to stronger and more durable relationships. It indicates your dedication to understanding and working through issues together.

4. Emotional Safety: When you manage arguments with care, you create a safe emotional atmosphere where women feel comfortable expressing their thoughts and emotions.

Effective Strategies for Handling Disagreements:

1 Active Listening: Start by listening closely to the other person's perspective. Show that you appreciate their views by giving them your entire attention and avoiding interruptions.

2. Empathetic Response: Acknowledge their feelings and perspective. Express empathy and compassion, even if you disagree. Phrases such as "I see how you are feeling" affirm their emotions.

3. Stay Calm: Maintain a calm and composed manner. Avoid raising your voice or resorting to violent language. A calm approach sets the stage for a more sensible discussion.

4. Utilize "I" phrases:When expressing your views, utilize "I" phrases to describe your feelings and thoughts without blaming the other person. For example, say, "I see it differently," don't say "You're wrong."

5. Seek mutual ground: Look for areas of agreement or mutual goals. This can help bridge the divide and facilitate compromise.

6. Stay Solution-Oriented: Focus on finding solutions rather than concentrating on the issue

itself. Collaborative problem-solving can be a unifying experience.

7. Respect Boundaries: Be cognizant of personal boundaries and comfort levels. If the other person needs space or time to process, respect their needs.

8. Take a Break When Necessary: If emotions run high and a debate becomes unproductive, it's fair to take a break and resume the issue later, when both sides are calmer and more attentive.

9. Learn from conflicts: View conflicts as chances for growth and learning. Even if you don't achieve a resolution, you can obtain a deeper understanding of the other person's perspective.

10. Apologize and Forgive: When appropriate, offer an apology if you discover you've made a mistake. Likewise, be ready to forgive and move forward when the other person apologizes.

Remember that the purpose of addressing disagreements is not always to "win" the argument but to maintain respect, understand one another better, and establish common ground where possible. As you traverse the art of explanation for women, the manner in which you manage differences plays a significant role in developing open and respectful communication.

Problem-Solving Strategies

Problem-solving is a critical ability in both personal and professional life, and learning effective ways to resolve challenges is particularly important when talking with women. Problem-solving not only helps address difficulties but also fosters teamwork and strengthens connections. Here's why it's vital and how to handle it effectively:

The Importance of Problem-Solving Strategies:

1 Resolution of Conflicts: Effective problem-solving is vital for resolving conflicts and disagreements in a productive manner.

It ensures that conflicts don't fester and severely influence relationships.

2. Achieving Goals: Problem-solving helps people and groups work together to achieve common goals. It permits the discovery and eradication of impediments on the route to success.

3. Innovation and Growth: Problem-solving often leads to inventive solutions and personal growth. It stimulates creativity and flexibility, establishing a culture of continual progress.

4. Enhanced Communication: Problem-solving tactics require active listening, empathy, and effective communication. This not only aids in addressing the subject at hand but also increases the quality of discourse.

Effective problem-solving strategies:

1 Define the problem: Clearly articulate the problem, its breadth, and its impact. Ensure everyone involved has a shared understanding of the situation.

2. Collaborative Approach: Problem-solving is most effective when done cooperatively. Involve all essential parties, including women, in the process.

3. Active Listening: Listen actively to the viewpoints and concerns of others. This entails hearing and appreciating the emotions and opinions of the people concerned.

4. Objective Analysis: Assess the problem objectively. Avoid making assumptions or judgments without proper evidence.

5. Generate Solutions: Encourage the production of multiple solutions. Creativity is often crucial to developing effective resolutions.

6. Evaluate Options: Consider the advantages and cons of each alternative. Evaluate which option is most likely to fix the problem and align with the goals of everyone concerned.

7. Seek Feedback: Invite feedback from all stakeholders. Ensure that the proposed solutions are agreeable to everyone, if possible.

8. Select and Implement: Choose the most suitable option and design an action plan for implementation. Define roles and duties.

9. Monitor Progress: Regularly monitor the progress of the chosen solution. Adapt or change the plan if necessary.

10. Closure and Reflection: Once the problem is resolved, take time for closure and reflection. Learn from the experience and examine ways to prevent such difficulties in the future.

11. Maintain Respect: Throughout the problem-solving process, maintain respect and open communication. Avoid blame or personal assaults.

12. Applaud Achievements: Recognize and celebrate the effective resolution of the problem and the combined work of the individuals concerned.

Problem-solving is a skill that can be polished and refined over time. When communicating with women, approach challenges with sensitivity and an open mind, taking into account their opinions and needs. Effective problem-solving not only leads to better solutions but also maintains a culture of cooperation and mutual respect in your relationships.

The Importance of Compromise

Compromise is a vital ingredient of effective communication and teamwork. It has a crucial role in settling problems, fostering healthy relationships, and accomplishing common goals. Understanding the need for compromise is particularly crucial when speaking with women, as it contributes to fostering an environment of understanding and respect. Here's why compromise is important and how to accept it:

The Significance of Compromise:

1 Conflict settlement: Compromise is a significant tool in conflict settlement. It permits individuals with opposing ideas or needs to find common ground and work together to address difficulties constructively.

2. Respect for Multiple Perspectives: Embracing compromise promotes respect for multiple perspectives and respects the significance of other viewpoints, especially when talking with women from varying backgrounds and experiences.

3. Fostering Collaboration: Compromise enhances collaboration and cooperation. It promotes teamwork and a shared commitment to finding solutions.

4. Maintaining Relationships: In personal and professional relationships, compromise is crucial for maintaining harmony and trust. It prevents arguments from growing and causing long-term damage to the partnership.

Embracing Compromise Effectively:

1 Open Communication: Begin by honestly discussing the subject at hand. Encourage everyone engaged to communicate their thoughts, needs, and expectations.

2. Active Listening: Actively listen to the opinions of others, taking into account their feelings and concerns. Show empathy and understanding.

3. Identify common aims: Look for shared aims and areas of agreement. These can serve as a platform for compromise and collaboration.

4. Provide Alternatives: Brainstorm and provide alternative ideas that consider the interests and preferences of all parties. Aim to discover a solution that is mutually agreeable.

5. Avoid rigidity: Be flexible and open to modifying your initial position.

Compromise often demands some give-and-take, and rigidity can inhibit development.

6. Value the Process: Understand that the process of compromise is as important as the ultimate outcome. It encourages respect, teamwork, and effective communication.

7. Seek win-win solutions: Strive for solutions that benefit all parties concerned, rather than favoring one side over the other. A win-win approach develops connections and encourages future cooperation.

8. Maintain Respect: Maintain respect and decency throughout the compromise process. Avoid personal assaults or discrediting the opinions of others.

9. Recognize the Bigger Picture: Consider the long-term benefits of compromise, not just the immediate resolution of the issue. Compromise can lead to healthier relationships and increased problem-solving skills.

10. Reflect and learn: After reaching a compromise, take time to reflect on the event and what you've learned from it. This self-awareness can increase your future communication and collaboration.

Understanding the significance of compromise and applying it in your interactions, especially when interacting with women, can lead to more courteous, productive, and harmonious partnerships. Compromise is a vital tool in the art of explaining and establishing a culture of cooperation and mutual understanding.

COMMUNICATING IN RELATIONSHIPS

Communication In Romantic Relationships

Effective communication is the cornerstone of any successful romantic connection. It is the glue that ties two individuals together, allowing them to comprehend one another, overcome issues, and cultivate a connection. In this section, we investigate the vital role that communication plays in romantic relationships and how it contributes to love, trust, and lasting bonds.

The Role of Communication in Romantic Relationships:

1 Building Connection: Communication is the bridge that unites two individuals on an emotional, intellectual, and spiritual level. Sharing thoughts, dreams, and vulnerabilities improves the emotional bond.

2. Understanding and Empathy: In love partnerships, partners generally come from various backgrounds and have unique viewpoints. Effective communication allows you to understand and empathize with your partner's experiences, even when they differ from your own.

3. Conflict Resolution: Disagreements are inherent in any relationship. Effective communication offers couples the tools to confront disputes respectfully, find solutions, and improve their bond in the process.

Closeness and Affection: Open and honest communication creates closeness and affection. Expressing love and want, as well as expressing desires and boundaries, deepens the physical and emotional connection.

Trust and Transparency: Trust is the foundation of a strong romantic connection. Communication fosters trust by establishing transparency and honesty in sharing thoughts and feelings.

Guidelines for Effective Communication in Romantic Relationships:

Active Listening: Pay complete attention when your companion speaks. Show that you are really interested in their opinions and feelings.

Empathetic Reactions: Show your partner that you understand and are sensitive to their feelings. Respect their emotions and give credence to what they've experienced.

Honesty and Transparency: Be honest and transparent in your conversation. Avoid holding secrets or hiding crucial facts.

Vulnerability: Open up and share your true self, including your fears, hopes, and insecurities. Vulnerability is a strong tool for creating trust and closeness.

Respect Boundaries: Respect your partner's personal boundaries and comfort levels. Not all topics need to be discussed immediately, and everyone deserves personal space.

Regular Check-Ins: Make a routine of checking in with each other to address the state of the relationship, any problems, or changes in feelings.

Quality Time:Dedicate quality time for important talks. Turn off distractions and emphasize spending time together to connect.

Positive Communication: Frame your words in a positive and productive manner.

Express your affection, appreciation, and concerns with kindness.

Resolve problems Constructively: When problems develop, address them calmly and constructively. Avoid personal attacks and work together to discover answers.

Common Goals and Future Plans: Discuss your common goals, aspirations, and future plans as a pair. It strengthens the idea of a shared trip.

Understanding the importance of communication in romantic relationships and applying these recommendations can help you have a deeper, more loving, and more enduring connection with your spouse. Effective communication is the key to negotiating the complexity of love and developing a relationship that stands the test of time.

Communication with friends and family

Effective communication with friends and family is the core of good and durable relationships. These are the people with whom you share your pleasures, challenges, and cherished moments. In this section, we discuss the value of communication in these relationships and how it contributes to understanding, support, and lasting bonds.

The Role of Communication with Friends and Family:

Connection and Understanding: Communication is the medium through which you connect with friends and family on an emotional and intimate level. It permits you to grasp their experiences, thoughts, and feelings.

Support and Empathy: In moments of joy or suffering, good communication provides a medium for sharing and receiving support and empathy. It strengthens the idea that you are not alone in your experiences.

Conflict Resolution: Disagreements and disagreements are inherent in any relationship. Communication is the tool that helps you resolve these concerns, discover common ground, and strengthen the link.

Celebration of Milestones: Communication is also the channel via which you share and celebrate major milestones, achievements, and special occasions in each other's lives.

Cultural and Family Traditions: Communicating within a family or social group typically entails the passing down of cultural and family traditions, beliefs, and wisdom from one generation to the next.Friends

Guidelines for Effective Communication with and Family:

Active Listening: Practice active listening while your friends or family members speak. Show that you are entirely involved and interested in what they have to say.

Empathetic Responses: Respond to their emotions with empathy and wisdom. Let them know that you acknowledge their feelings and experiences.

Honesty and openness: Honesty is vital to your connection with loved ones. Be transparent about your views and feelings, and urge them to do the same.

Vulnerability: Don't be scared to be vulnerable with friends and family. Share your concerns, hopes, and insecurities, which can generate deeper connections.

Respect Boundaries: Respect personal boundaries and comfort levels. Understand that not everyone is ready to discuss every topic or emotion at all times.

Quality Time: Dedicate quality time to spend with friends and family, ensuring that you have space for meaningful conversations and shared experiences.

Conflict Resolution: When disagreements emerge, address them with a focus on resolution rather than winning an argument. Find common ground and compromise as needed.

Celebration and Appreciation: Express your affection, appreciation, and congratulations on their successes and key life events.

Shared Traditions and Stories: Keep alive your family and cultural traditions and stories. Share them with younger generations to pass on ideals and memories.

Regular Check-Ins: Make regular check-ins part of your communication pattern to guarantee you stay connected and current on each other's lives.

Effective communication with friends and family adds to stronger relationships, deeper understanding, and an enduring support network. It strengthens the links that hold you together through the ups and downs of life and underlines the importance of shared experiences and connections with those you hold dear.

Building Stronger Connections

Strong connections with others are the foundation of a full and meaningful life. Whether it's in personal relationships, friendships, or professional networks, the ability to develop and sustain strong connections is a crucial skill. In this section, we explore the significance of strong connections and how to develop them effectively.

The Significance of Building Stronger Connections:

Emotional Support: Strong connections are a source of emotional support, helping individuals traverse life's problems with a sense of stability and understanding.

Enhanced Well-Being: Research repeatedly reveals that strong social ties are associated with enhanced mental and physical well-being. They alleviate tension and boost happiness.

Professional Growth: In a professional environment, good connections can open doors to new opportunities, partnerships, and career advancement.

Shared Experiences: Building better connections allows you to exchange experiences, ideas, and perspectives, enriching your life with varied viewpoints.

Trust and Reliability: Strong ties are formed on trust and reliability. You can depend on one another, establishing a sense of safety and security.

Guidelines for Building Stronger Connections:

1 Active Listening: Practice active listening in your conversations. Show that you are fully present and engaged in what the other person is saying.

2. Empathy: Cultivate empathy and understanding for the feelings and experiences of others. Put yourself in their shoes to better comprehend their perspective.

3. Quality Time: Dedicate quality time to spend with people you wish to connect with. This fosters meaningful interactions and shared experiences.

4. Open and honest conversation: Be open and honest in your conversation. Sharing your thoughts and feelings might lead to deeper connections.

5. Vulnerability: Don't be frightened to be vulnerable. Sharing your concerns, hopes, and insecurities can establish deeper and more honest friendships.

6. Respect Boundaries: Respect personal boundaries and comfort levels. Everyone has their own timetable for creating connections, so be considerate.

7. Common Activities: Engage in common activities and experiences. This fosters a sense of connection and shared memories.

8. Support and Encouragement: Provide support and encouragement when needed. Be present for people in moments of success and struggle.

9. Thanks: Express your thanks and thankfulness for the relationship. Acknowledge the value the other person offers to your life.

10. Consistency: Consistency is crucial in developing stronger bonds. Regularly check in and maintain your connections to keep them bright and healthy.

11. Forgiveness: Be ready to forgive and move on when conflicts or misunderstandings occur. Forgiveness is often an aspect of strengthening ties.

12. Shared Goals: Discover and work toward shared goals and aspirations. Building something together can enhance your connection.

Building greater connections is an ongoing process that requires work and a genuine desire to understand and appreciate others. As you explore the art of explanation in all parts of your life, remember that the quality of your connections can profoundly affect your pleasure, well-being, and personal and professional growth.

WORKPLACE COMMUNICATION

Women In The Professional World

The role of women in the working sphere has developed greatly throughout the years, and it continues to undergo revolutionary changes. In this section, we'll analyze the problems, developments, and relevance of supporting women in the professional sector.

Challenges Faced by Women in the Professional World:

1 Gender Bias: Gender bias, typically in the form of preconceptions and preconceived notions, can inhibit women's development on the job.

2. Pay Inequality: The gender pay gap remains in many industries, with women earning less than their male counterparts for the same work.

3. Underrepresentation: Women are underrepresented in leadership roles and particular fields, resulting in a lack of diverse perspectives in decision-making.

4. Work-Life Balance: Balancing professional and family commitments is sometimes tough for women, especially in environments without supportive regulations.

Progress and Achievements:

1 Increased Representation: Women have made considerable achievements in assuming professions that were formerly male-dominated,

such as science, technology, engineering, and mathematics (STEM) fields.

2. Legislation: Legal measures, including anti-discrimination laws and family leave policies, have been enacted to safeguard and support women's rights in the workplace.

3. Empowerment: Women's networks, mentorship programs, and initiatives have enabled women to achieve leadership positions and contribute to good change.

4. Awareness and activism: There is increased awareness and activism for gender equality, with many groups and individuals working to promote equal opportunities for women.

The Importance of Supporting Women in the Professional World:

1 varied perspectives: A varied workforce, including women, adds to richer and more imaginative decision-making, problem-solving, and creativity.

2. Economic Growth: Empowering women in the workforce can contribute greatly to economic growth and prosperity by tapping into a larger talent pool.

3. Social Progress: Gender equality in the workplace is a significant component of larger societal progress and the struggle against discrimination and injustice.

4. Personal Fulfillment: For individual women, professional achievement and fulfillment can lead to a higher quality of life and personal happiness.

Supporting women in the professional sector requires fostering inclusive workplaces, ensuring equitable opportunities, addressing salary discrepancies, and overcoming gender biases. It's about understanding that everyone, regardless of their gender, should have the chance to accomplish their career objectives and contribute their abilities to society. As you engage in the art of explanation, explore the significance of gender equality and how it might positively impact professional contexts and society at large.

Effective communication at work

Effective communication in the workplace is crucial to success, whether you're working with colleagues, superiors, or subordinates. It's a skill that fosters teamwork, minimizes misunderstandings, and promotes a healthy work atmosphere. In this section, we'll cover the necessity of effective communication at work and techniques to master it.

The Importance of Effective Communication at Work:

1   Clarity   and   Understanding: Clear communication   ensures   that   everyone understands their roles, responsibilities, and objectives. This clarity minimizes errors and misunderstandings.

2. Teamwork and cooperation: Effective communication is crucial for teamwork and cooperation. It facilitates the exchange of ideas, criticism, and productive conversations.

3. Conflict Resolution: Inevitably, disagreements develop   in   the   workplace.   Effective communication enables the settlement of these problems in a polite and constructive manner.

4. Employee Engagement: When employees feel heard and respected, their engagement and job satisfaction increase. Effective communication generates a positive work atmosphere.

5.   Innovation   and   Problem-Solving: Encouraging open communication leads to the exchange of new ideas and problem-solving, which can benefit the business as a whole.

Strategies for Effective Communication at Work:

1 Active Listening: Pay close attention to what people are saying and indicate that you are fully engaged in the conversation by making eye contact, nodding, and asking clarifying questions.

2. Clarity and Conciseness: Be clear and succinct in your message. Avoid jargon or complex explanations. Get to the point to ensure understanding.

3. Empathetic Responses: Show empathy and understanding in your responses. Acknowledge the feelings and concerns of your colleagues.

4. Open Communication Channels: Create an environment where employees feel comfortable discussing their opinions and concerns. Encourage feedback and open communication.

5. Respect and civility: Treat coworkers with respect and civility in all dealings. Avoid insulting language or actions.

6. Written Communication: In written communication, be attentive to grammar and tone. Proofread your messages to guarantee clarity and professionalism.

7. Conflict Resolution Skills: Learn how to manage disagreement constructively. Focus on seeking solutions rather than casting blame.

8. Adapt to Different Styles: Recognize that people have different communication styles. Adapt to the preferences of your coworkers to promote good communication.

9. Meetings with a Purpose: Conduct meetings with a defined agenda and purpose. Keep them focused and ensure that all participants have an opportunity to contribute.

10. Feedback Culture: Create a culture of regular feedback. Encourage employees to submit feedback to one another and to management.

11. Professional Development: Invest in professional development to improve your communication abilities, which can improve your employment possibilities.

Effective communication at work is a talent that can be learned and perfected over time. It adds to a peaceful work atmosphere, encourages professional growth, and enhances job satisfaction. As you traverse the art of explanation in your professional life, remember that excellent communication skills are a vital tool.

Navigating Office Dynamics

Office dynamics relate to the interactions, relationships, and unwritten conventions that create the workplace environment. It's crucial to navigate these dynamics successfully to foster a happy and productive work climate. In this section, we'll cover the significance of recognizing and managing office dynamics and present suggestions for success.

The Significance of Navigating Office Dynamics:

1 Productivity and Collaboration: A peaceful workplace encourages collaboration and develops productivity. Understanding office dynamics is crucial to achieving this equilibrium.

2. Conflict Resolution: Inevitably, disagreements develop in the workplace. Navigating office dynamics means handling these disputes constructively and limiting their impact.

3. Career Growth: Successfully handling office dynamics can provide avenues for career growth and progress. It's often about creating great relationships and earning the trust of coworkers and superiors.

4. Job Satisfaction: A positive work environment contributes to job satisfaction and general well-being. Navigating office dynamics can enrich your job experience.

Strategies for Navigating Office Dynamics:

1 Examine and learn: Take the time to examine the present office dynamics. Learn from

seasoned colleagues and comprehend the unwritten standards and expectations.

2. Good Communication: Practice good communication by being straightforward, respectful, and receptive to feedback. Active listening is a primary component of good communication.

3. Build Positive Relationships: Invest in building productive relationships with friends. Treat other people with respect, meekness and professionalism.

4. Conflict resolution abilities: Develop abilities for resolving disagreements constructively. Focus on finding solutions and retaining respect, especially during conflicts.

5. Adaptability: Be adaptive and open to change. The workplace is dynamic, and flexibility is an asset in negotiating altering office dynamics.

6. Professional limits: Maintain professional limits. Avoid becoming embroiled in office politics or gossip that might be bad for your reputation.

7. Teamwork and Collaboration: Encourage teamwork and collaboration. Be a team player who supports the collective aims of the organization.

8. Leadership Skills: If you have a leadership role, acquire leadership skills that support favorable workplace dynamics, including effective communication, problem-solving, and empathy.

9. Self-Awareness: Develop self-awareness to comprehend how your actions and behaviors affect workplace dynamics. Be receptive to self-improvement.

10. Mentorship and direction: Seek mentorship or direction from experienced colleagues or supervisors who can provide useful insights into office dynamics.

11. Maintain a Positive Attitude: A positive attitude can have a big impact on office dynamics. Approach issues with a problem-solving mindset.

Understanding and successfully navigating office dynamics is a constant process that requires self-awareness, emotional intelligence, and adaptation. It adds not only to your professional advancement but also to the overall well-being of the workplace. As you study the art of explanation in your profession, remember that the ability to negotiate office dynamics is a crucial talent that can open doors to chances and success.

DIGITAL COMMUNICATION AND SOCIAL MEDIA

Communication In The Digital Age

The digital age has brought about a shift in how we communicate, connect, and share information. It has transformed the way we engage with one another in both personal and professional circumstances. In this section, we'll discuss the influence of digital communication and the skills essential to navigate this new world effectively.

The Impact of Digital Communication:

1 Instant Connectivity: Digital technology enables us to connect instantly with people across the globe, promoting conversation in real time.

2. Information Sharing: Digital platforms have become effective instruments for sharing information, ideas, and material with a wide audience.

3. Distant Work: The growth of digital communication tools has made distant work and collaboration possible, revolutionizing the way we conduct business.

4. Global Reach: Digital communication transcends geographical boundaries, allowing individuals and organizations to communicate with a global audience.

5. obstacles: The digital age poses obstacles, including information overload, privacy concerns, and the need to traverse a broad and changing array of platforms and tools.

Skills for Proper Communication in the Digital Age:

1 Digital Literacy: Develop digital literacy abilities to efficiently use numerous communication technologies, including email, social media, and messaging applications.

2. Email Etiquette: Practice proper email etiquette, which encompasses clear and succinct messages, appropriate subject lines, and professionalism.

3. Social Media Awareness: Understand the influence of social media and utilize it properly, considering its potential consequences for personal and professional life.

4. Online Security: Be aware of online security procedures to protect your personal information and privacy.

5. Effective Material Creation: Learn to generate engaging and useful material that resonates with your target audience.

6. Adaptability: Stay open to new communication methods and trends. Adaptability is very important in the ever-evolving digital space.

7. Balanced Use: Practice balanced digital use, cognizant of the potential for digital addiction and its influence on mental health and well-being.

8. Online Networking: Utilize online networking platforms for career advancement, developing professional relationships, and staying updated on industry trends.

9. Media Literacy: Develop media literacy abilities to critically analyze information sources and identify credible content from falsehoods.

10. Time Management: Effectively manage your digital time to enhance productivity and decrease distractions.

11. Cybersecurity Awareness: Learn about cybersecurity methods to protect against online threats and data breaches.

12. Digital Empathy: Extend empathy and kindness in your online encounters, realizing that digital communication should be just as respectful as face-to-face conversation.

The digital age has revolutionized the way we communicate, presenting amazing opportunities and problems. By learning the required skills and knowledge, individuals can embrace the power of digital communication for personal and professional progress while limiting its potential hazards. In your path of explaining, understanding, and connecting with others, it's crucial to embrace the digital world and the opportunities it brings for communication and collaboration.

Social media and online etiquette

In the digital age, social media and internet platforms have become vital components of our personal and professional lives. Navigating these digital environments with decorum and courtesy is vital for sustaining great relationships, protecting your online reputation, and utilizing the potential of these platforms. In this section, we'll cover the importance of social media and online etiquette and present recommendations for safe and respectful online communication.

The Importance of Social Media and Online Etiquette:

1 Online Reputation: Your online behavior can substantially affect your personal and professional reputation. What you post and how you connect with people reflect on you.

2. connections: Respectful online behavior is crucial for nurturing and maintaining connections with friends, family, colleagues, and acquaintances.

3. Professionalism: In a professional context, preserving internet decorum is vital for career advancement, networking, and representing your organization professionally.

4. Avoiding Misunderstandings: Online communication can be readily misconstrued. Practicing proper etiquette helps minimize misunderstandings and disputes.

Guidelines for Social Media and Online Etiquette:

1 Respect Others: Treat others with respect, kindness, and decency, just as you would in face-to-face conversations. Avoid rude or aggressive words.

2. Think Before You Post: Before sharing content or making comments, consider the potential influence on your reputation and connections. Is it appropriate and in accordance with your values?

3. Privacy Settings: Review and update your privacy settings to manage who may see your posts and personal information.

4. Fact-check: Verify the accuracy of information before sharing it. Avoid disseminating inaccurate or misleading content.

5. Mindful Posting: Be mindful of what you post, especially when addressing sensitive themes like politics, religion, or contentious problems. Engage in constructive discourse rather than angry arguments.

6. Positive Content: Share positive and constructive content that gives value to the online community. Encourage and assist others.

7. Be responsive: acknowledge and respond to comments or communications in a timely manner. Ignoring or disregarding online conversations might be regarded as impolite.

8. Protect Personal Information: Be cautious about sharing personal information, such as addresses, phone numbers, or financial details, in public posts or with unfamiliar individuals.

9. Respect Copyright: Respect copyright rules when sharing content. Give proper credit to the creators and get permission when necessary.

10. Online Tone: Pay attention to your tone in written communication. Text can lack the context offered by facial expressions and voice cues, so ensure your tone is clear and courteous.

11. Handle Criticism Gracefully: When faced with criticism or unpleasant comments, reply with grace and professionalism. Address issues and engage in meaningful discourse.

12. Regularly Review Profiles: Periodically review your social media profiles to verify that they match your current beliefs and aspirations. Update old or irrelevant content.

Practicing social media and internet etiquette is not just a matter of respect but also a reflection of your character and ideals. It can drastically affect your personal and professional connections; therefore, it's crucial to be cautious of your online activity. As you engage in digital communication and explanation, remember that appropriate and respectful online etiquette is an essential skill for the digital age.

Maintaining Healthy Digital Relationships

In today's digital age, our relationships extend beyond face-to-face contacts, and it's vital to ensure that these digital ties remain healthy and happy. Whether it's with friends, family, or professional contacts, sustaining strong digital interactions includes balancing online communication with decency, respect, and accountability. In this section, we'll explore the significance of healthy digital relationships and present tips for cultivating them.

The Significance of Healthy Digital Relationships:

1 Connection: Healthy digital relationships help us stay connected with loved ones, no matter where they are in the world.

2. Professional Growth: In a professional environment, digital contacts are crucial for networking, cooperation, and career advancement.

3. Help: These ties provide emotional and practical help in times of need, providing a sense of community and belonging.

4. Communication: Effective digital connections depend on clear, polite, and responsible communication.

Guidelines for Maintaining Healthy Digital Relationships:

1 Set limits: Establish digital limits to ensure a healthy balance between online and offline life. Limit screen time and focus on in-person interactions when possible.

2. Respect Response Times: Be patient and sensitive about response times. Not everyone can reply promptly, and people have various schedules and obligations.

3. Clear Communication: Practice clear and polite communication. Use suitable language and tone in your messages, whether they are through text, email, or social media.

4. Respect Privacy: Respect the privacy and limitations of your digital contacts. Avoid disclosing their personal details without permission.

5. Online Support: Provide emotional support and encouragement to others in your digital community when they need it. Offer a listening ear or words of kindness.

6. Use emojis deliberately. Emojis can convey emotions and tone, but use them deliberately to avoid misunderstandings.

7. Conflict Resolution: Address conflicts or misunderstandings constructively. Engage in open and polite discourse to identify solutions.

8. Digital Empathy: Practice digital empathy by considering the sentiments and views of the people you deal with online.

9. Avoid Digital Neglect: Don't allow digital communication to replace face-to-face contact. Make an effort to spend time with loved ones in person when possible.

10. Periodic Check-Ins: Make an effort to check in with your digital contacts periodically, even if it's just a simple note to indicate you care.

11. Create healthy online behaviors: Encourage your digital contacts to create healthy online behaviors, such as regulating screen time and avoiding cyberbullying.

12. Share Positivity: Share positive and uplifting content and contribute to a positive online environment.

Healthy digital connections are defined by respect, responsibility, and emotional support. They add value to our lives and contribute to our general well-being. As you engage in the art of explanation and connect with others in the digital arena, remember that the quality of your digital relationships is a reflection of your kindness, respect, and care for others.

UNDERSTANDING FEMALE PERSPECTIVES

Breaking Stereotypes

Stereotypes are preconceived conceptions and simplistic opinions about people based on their features, such as gender, race, age, or social background. These preconceptions can lead to misunderstanding, discrimination, and prejudice. Breaking preconceptions is a vital step toward developing understanding, inclusivity, and unity in our diverse world. In this section, we'll explore the importance of breaking stereotypes and present ways for confronting and overcoming them.

The Significance of Breaking Stereotypes:

1   Promoting   Inclusivity: Breaking preconceptions is crucial for fostering inclusive communities and workplaces where everyone is appreciated and respected.

2. Reducing prejudice: Stereotypes can contribute to prejudice and bias. Challenging these assumptions is vital for developing a fair and just society.

3. Fostering Empathy: Breaking stereotypes helps individuals develop empathy and a deeper understanding of the experiences and views of others.

4. Enhancing Relationships: Stereotypes can hurt relationships and communication. Overcoming them can lead to stronger, more respectful interactions.

Strategies for breaking stereotypes:

1 Self-Reflection: Start by assessing your own assumptions and biases. Recognize where you might hold stereotypes and resolve to change.

2. Education: Seek to educate yourself about diverse cultures, backgrounds, and opinions. Read, attend workshops, and engage with varied groups.

3. Empathetic Listening: Listen to the experiences of those who have been touched by stereotypes. Show empathy and understanding.

4. Challenge Assumptions: Question your assumptions and generalizations about individuals. Approach each individual as unique, rather than a reflection of a group.

5. Diversity and Inclusion: Promote diversity and inclusion in your personal and professional settings. Encourage varied viewpoints and voices.

6. Be an Ally: Stand up against stereotypes and bigotry when you witness them. Be an ally to those who encounter stereotypes.

7. Language Matters: Be cautious of the language you use. Avoid disparaging phrases and stereotypes that foster bias.

8. Avoid generalizations: Refrain from making generalizations about large groups of people. Instead, focus on individuals and their distinct features.

9. Media Literacy: Develop media literacy skills to critically examine the portrayal of different groups in media and popular culture.

10. Cultural Exchange: Engage in cultural exchange and engagement with people from varied backgrounds. This can remove preconceptions and develop connections.

11. Teach and Model: If you are a parent or educator, teach the next generation about the impact of stereotypes and the conduct that confronts them.

12. Encourage discourse: Promote open and polite discourse about stereotypes and their influence in your community or workplace.

Breaking stereotypes is an ongoing effort that involves self-awareness, education, and a dedication to creating a more inclusive and empathic environment. As you study the art of explanation and understanding, remember that by challenging stereotypes and fostering inclusivity, you contribute to a more just and harmonious society where every individual is valued for their unique talents and potential.

Intersectionality and Diversity

Intersectionality is a concept that recognizes the linked nature of multiple parts of a person's identity, such as race, gender, sexual orientation, financial class, and more. Understanding intersectionality is vital for appreciating the richness of individuals' experiences and for fostering diversity and inclusion. In this section, we'll study the relevance of intersectionality and diversity and how these concepts interact to build a more equal society.

The Significance of Intersectionality:

1 Complex Identities: Intersectionality emphasizes that individuals have complex and multiple identities, which shape their experiences and viewpoints.

2. Inequality and Discrimination: People at the crossroads of many identities may encounter compounded experiences of discrimination and bigotry.

3. Diverse viewpoints: Recognizing intersectionality leads to a deeper awareness of variety, allowing for a richer tapestry of viewpoints and voices.

4. Inclusive Solutions: It's crucial for generating inclusive solutions and policies that address the particular issues encountered by individuals with intersecting identities.

The Importance of Diversity:

1 Broadening viewpoints: Diversity increases the pool of viewpoints and ideas, supporting innovation, creativity, and problem-solving.

2. Inclusivity: Promoting diversity ensures that everyone has a seat at the table, generating a sense of belonging and inclusivity.

3. Fairness and Equality: A varied and inclusive society promotes fairness and equality, combating discrimination and bias.

4. Empowering marginalized perspectives: Diversity strengthens individuals from marginalized communities and amplifies their perspectives and contributions.

Strategies for Promoting Intersectionality and Diversity:

1 Education and Awareness: Educate yourself about intersectionality and the experiences of individuals with multiple identities.

2. Representation: Advocate for varied representation in all sectors of life, including media, politics, and employment.

3. Inclusive Language: Use inclusive language that respects people's identities and pronouns and avoids assumptions.

4. Anti-Discrimination Measures: Support anti-discrimination policies and efforts that promote equity and inclusion.

5. Empower Marginalized Groups: Empower and raise the voices of persons from marginalized communities. Listen to their experiences and stories.

6. Cultural Competency: Develop cultural competency and sensitivity to other backgrounds and experiences.

7. Challenge Stereotypes: Challenge stereotypes and biases that may lead to discrimination.

8. Promote Inclusive Practices: Encourage companies and institutions to adopt inclusive practices in hiring, promotion, and decision-making.

9. Intersectional Solutions: Advocate for policies and solutions that reflect intersectionality and the specific needs of individuals with intersecting identities.

10. Allyship: Be an ally to people who may be facing prejudice or bias due to their overlapping identities.

Promoting intersectionality and diversity is an ongoing and collective effort that benefits society as a whole.

By understanding and respecting the complexity of people's identities and building inclusive and diverse surroundings, we may move towards a more equitable and harmonious society. In your journey of explanation and understanding, explore the importance of these principles in creating a society where every individual's unique experiences are acknowledged and cherished.

The Power of Inclusivity

Inclusivity is a key idea that supports the equitable participation and contribution of all people, regardless of their differences, in all parts of society. It is a force that builds communities, organizations, and societies by appreciating and honoring the unique viewpoints and experiences of each person. In this section, we'll discuss the relevance of inclusion and how it can positively impact numerous facets of our lives.

The Significance of Inclusivity:

1 Diverse viewpoints: Inclusivity invites diverse viewpoints, ideas, and experiences to the table, boosting innovation, creativity, and problem-solving.

2. Fairness and Justice: An inclusive society works for fairness and justice, addressing prejudice and injustice based on race, gender, sexual orientation, age, and other criteria.

3. Empowerment: Inclusivity strengthens underprivileged groups and individuals by giving them a voice and ensuring they are heard and valued.

4. Belonging: Inclusivity generates a sense of belonging, where every individual feels appreciated and accepted for who they are.

The Power of Inclusivity:

1 Fosters Creativity: Inclusivity encourages varied perspectives, which can lead to more innovative solutions and creative thinking.

2. Strengthens Communities: Inclusive communities are frequently more resilient and supportive, fostering a sense of unity and solidarity.

3. Promotes Learning: Inclusivity contributes to higher educational outcomes by recognizing and accommodating varied learning styles and demands.

4. Enhances Workplace Productivity: Inclusive organizations frequently have higher employee satisfaction, leading to increased productivity and retention.

5. Cultural Enrichment: Inclusivity brings together people from many cultural origins, enriching society with different traditions, art, and ideas.

Strategies for Promoting Inclusivity:

1 Education and Awareness: Raise awareness about the need for inclusivity and educate yourself and others about other identities and experiences.

2. Representation: Advocate for diverse representation in leadership, media, and decision-making roles.

3. Inclusive Language: Use language that respects people's identities, pronouns, and experiences, and avoid making assumptions.

4. Anti-Discrimination Measures: Support anti-discrimination policies and efforts that promote equity and inclusion.

5. Empower marginalized voices: amplify the voices and contributions of people from marginalized communities. Listen to their stories and experiences.

6. Cultural Competency: Develop cultural competency and sensitivity to other backgrounds and experiences.

7. Challenge Stereotypes: Challenge stereotypes and biases that may lead to discrimination and exclusion.

8. Promote Inclusive Practices: Encourage companies and institutions to adopt inclusive practices in hiring, promotion, and decision-making.

Inclusivity is a powerful force that can lead to stronger, more inventive, and more equitable societies.

By acknowledging and respecting the unique viewpoints and experiences of each person, we can build a world where every person is valued and included. As you traverse the art of explanation and understanding, remember the transforming power of inclusivity and its ability to enrich our lives and our communities.

EMPOWERING WOMEN THROUGH COMMUNICATION

Building Confidence

Confidence is a fundamental attribute that helps individuals accept challenges, take chances, and pursue their goals. It is not an intrinsic quality but a skill that can be developed and strengthened over time. In this section, we'll explore the relevance of creating confidence and present ways for increasing this crucial quality.

The Significance of Building Confidence:

1 Personal Empowerment: Confidence encourages individuals to believe in their skills and take control of their lives.

2. Risk-Taking: Confident individuals are more willing to take calculated chances and pursue new opportunities.

3. Resilience: Confidence functions as a buffer against self-doubt and despair amid setbacks.

4. Effective Communication: Confidence provides improved communication and the capacity to express thoughts and ideas clearly.

5. Success: Confidence is often a vital aspect of obtaining personal and professional success.

Strategies for Building Confidence:

1 Self-acceptance: Accept yourself, including your strengths and weaknesses. Acknowledging flaws is the first step toward establishing confidence.

2. Set realistic goals: Set feasible goals and split them into smaller, doable steps. Each accomplishment develops confidence.

3. Positive Self-Talk: Challenge negative self-talk and replace it with positive affirmations and beliefs about your capabilities.

4. Competence Development: Acquire knowledge and skills in areas that interest you. Competence develops confidence.

5. Visualization: Visualize success and pleasant results in diverse scenarios. This can help alleviate anxiety and promote confidence.

6. Celebrate Achievements: Celebrate your successes, no matter how minor. Recognizing your achievements increases confidence.

7. Embrace Challenges: Welcome challenges as chances for growth. Facing difficulties and conquering obstacles strengthens confidence.

8. Learn from Failure: View failure as motivation to success. Learning from setbacks might improve confidence in future initiatives.

9. Body Language: Adopt confident body language, such as good posture and eye contact. It can influence how you feel and how others view you.

10. Seek Support: Surround yourself with supportive friends and mentors who encourage your growth and confidence.

11. Professional Development: Invest in professional development and education to expand your knowledge and skills in your chosen field.

12. Take action: Don't allow self-doubt to paralyze you. Take action, even if it means moving out of your comfort zone.

Building confidence is a lifetime endeavor that takes self-awareness and dedication to personal progress. It's about embracing challenges, learning from experiences, and continuously growing your abilities and self-belief. As you study the art of explanation and communicate with the world, remember that confidence is a precious commodity that can empower you to realize your full potential and achieve your goals.

Leadership and Communication

Effective communication is the basis of strong leadership. Whether you're leading a team, an organization, or a community, your ability to communicate clearly, inspire, and connect with others plays a crucial role in your success as a leader. In this section, we'll explore the significant connection between leadership and communication and share insights into how to become a more effective leader through communication.

The Significance of Leadership and Communication:

1 Inspiration: Leaders utilize communication to inspire and encourage their team or followers toward a common objective.

2. Clarity: Effective communication ensures that the vision, goals, and expectations are obvious to everyone involved.

3. Trust and Respect: Leaders develop trust and respect by communicating frankly and honestly.

4. Conflict Resolution: Communication skills help leaders resolve disagreements and problems in a positive manner.

5. Decision-Making: Effective leaders use communication to obtain information, share insights, and make informed decisions.

Strategies for Effective Leadership Communication:

1 Active Listening: Be an active listener. Pay attention to what people are saying, ask clarifying questions, and indicate that you value their viewpoint.

2. Clear Vision: Communicate a clear and compelling vision. Help people understand the goals and the role they play in accomplishing them.

3. Empathy: Practice empathy in your conversation. Understand the feelings and opinions of those you lead.

4. Feedback: Provide regular and constructive feedback to help individuals grow and improve.

5. Transparency: Be open and transparent about information and conclusions, even when discussing difficult topics.

6. Adapt to Your Audience: Tailor your communication style to your audience, realizing that various people have varied communication preferences.

7. Confidence: Communicate with confidence, expressing that you believe in the road forward.

8. Conflict resolution abilities: Develop abilities for resolving disagreements within the team or organization in a fair and courteous manner.

9. Inspire and Motivate: Use storytelling and inspirational language to motivate your staff and keep them interested.

10. Lead by example: Set the benchmark for communication by demonstrating the behavior you demand from your team.

11. Crisis Communication: Be prepared to communicate effectively under hard circumstances. Stay composed and provide reassurance when needed.

12. Continual Improvement: Regularly analyze your leadership communication and explore possibilities for improvement.

Leaders that thrive in communication not only deliver knowledge but also build a sense of trust, motivation, and belonging among their team or followers. They lead by example, establishing the tone for the business or community and helping others attain their full potential. As you traverse the art of explanation and leadership, remember that excellent communication is a crucial tool for motivating and encouraging those you lead.

Inspiring Change

Change is an inherent part of life and progress. Whether it's personal growth, organizational development, or societal advancement, inspiring change is a key aspect of leadership and influence. In this section, we'll explore the significance of inspiring change and provide strategies for effectively leading and motivating change processes.

The Significance of Inspiring Change:

1. Growth and Progress: Change is essential for growth, progress, and innovation in all aspects of life.

2. Adaptability: The ability to inspire and adapt to change is crucial in a rapidly evolving world.

3. Problem-Solving: Change often addresses problems and challenges, providing opportunities for improvement.

4. Leadership: Inspiring change is a hallmark of effective leadership, whether it's in a personal or professional context.

Strategies for Inspiring Change:

1. Clear Vision: Communicate a clear and compelling vision for the change. Help others understand the "why" and the benefits of the change.

2. Lead by Example: Demonstrate your commitment to the change by embodying the values and behaviors you expect from others.

3. Effective Communication: Use persuasive and inclusive communication to convey the necessity and positive aspects of the change.

4. Engage Stakeholders: Involve those affected by the change in the decision-making process. Listen to their concerns, and incorporate their feedback.

5. Provide Resources: Ensure that individuals have the resources, support, and training necessary to adapt to the change.

6. Set Realistic Goals: Break down the change into smaller, achievable goals. Celebrate small victories along the way.

7. Embrace Innovation: Encourage and embrace innovative ideas and approaches that can facilitate the change.

8. Resilience: Expect and address setbacks. Encourage perseverance and resilience in the face of obstacles.

9. Feedback Loops: Establish feedback mechanisms to continually assess the progress of the change and make necessary adjustments.

10. Celebrate Success: Celebrate milestones and successes to maintain motivation and reinforce the benefits of the change.

11. Crisis Management: Be prepared for resistance and conflict, and address challenges with a calm and constructive approach.

12. Lead with Empathy: Understand the feelings and concerns of those affected by the change. Show empathy and support.

Inspiring change is often met with resistance, but effective leadership can turn that resistance into motivation. By clearly communicating the need for change, involving stakeholders, providing support, and celebrating successes, you can inspire a sense of purpose and excitement about the transformations that lie ahead. As you navigate the art of explanation and influence, remember that inspiring change is a powerful force for progress and growth, both for yourself and those you lead.

CONCLUSION

As we raise the closing curtain on our examination of this book, we find ourselves at a junction where understanding, connection, and empathy have illuminated our path. This journey has been a voyage into the intricate world of communication, with a focus on the unique dynamics that can arise when women speak.

Throughout this book, we've explored the tapestry of human contact, uncovering the relevance of efficient communication in fostering better relationships and building bridges of understanding. We've looked into the intricacies of gender and communication, knowing that the key to good communication is embracing diversity and honoring unique opinions. We've covered the unseen language of nonverbal signs, the skill of developing rapport, and the power of expression, all of which play key roles in connecting with others.

We've learned how tone and word choice shape our communications, how to manage arguments respectfully, and how to utilize problem-solving skills to overcome problems. We've underlined the significance of compromise and covered communication in numerous scenarios, from love relationships to professional settings and the digital age. We've acknowledged the value of inclusivity, busting preconceptions, and supporting diversity, all of which improve our connections and understanding.

We've covered the value of gaining confidence, both for personal growth and leadership, and explored the skill of inspiring change, a force that drives progress and development. And we've realized the significant significance of maintaining healthy relationships, where empathy, respect, and communication come together to create a supportive and happy atmosphere.

In our last chapter, we've taken stock of the remarkable terrain we've covered. Each page, each chapter, has been a stepping stone toward a more thorough mastery of the art of explanation and the comprehension of the complexity of human communication, particularly when it involves women.

Through your interaction with this book, you've shown your commitment to strengthening your communication skills and understanding the complexities of human connection. As you push forward, realize that the process of communication mastery is ongoing. Every day brings a new opportunity to deepen your skills and develop more significant relationships.

May this book serve as a compass for navigating the convoluted world of communication with women and as a reminder that the mysteries of connection can indeed be uncovered.

As you implement the lessons learned and insights obtained, may your relationships be marked by respect, empathy, and a profound appreciation for the unique perspectives each person brings to the table.

Thank you for joining us on this informative adventure, and may your continuous search for communication mastery continue to enhance your life and the lives of people you connect with.